www.prolancewriting.com
California, USA

©2021 Islam4families.com

By Sahar Abdel-Aziz
Illustrated by Laila Ramadhani
Edited by Hadeer Soliman and Jenna Albaroudi

ISBN-13: 978-1-7371558-8-1
Printed in USA
All rights reserved. No part of the publication may be reproduced in any form without prior permission from the publisher.

PREFACE

In 1998, when Christmas, Hanukkah, and Ramadan were all celebrated during the month of December, I took my three children, then 9-year-old Hadeer, 8-year-old Siraj and 6-year-old Janna to Story Time at the local library.

With great excitement, the librarian told the wide-eyed children that she would read to them stories about the holidays taking place in December: Christmas and Hanukkah.

My daughter, Hadeer, almost automatically, said to me, "How about Ramadan, Mommy? That's in December, too."

After Story Time was over, I asked the librarian to share with the children a story about Ramadan because the holidays coincided this year.

The librarian responded, "Ramadan is not a fun month; it's religious."

I proceeded to tell her that, like Christmas and Hanukkah, Ramadan is also a religious time, and that it can, in fact, be fun, just like those two holidays.

After a long discussion on this matter, the librarian agreed. If I could bring her a children's story about Ramadan, she would share it during Story Time at the library.

Naturally, I looked in the library for a children's short story about Ramadan.

However, to my children's disappointment and mine, there were none.

That is when I began working with my children on building on their own experiences to write a story about Ramadan.

I also designed an art project for the children to participate in during Story Time the following week at the library.

Alhamdulilah, we were ready that week with a story to share with the children, and we made a lantern as the library's art project for the week.

The following year, when I started teaching and developing the Islamic Studies curriculum at New Horizon School in Los Angeles, Calif., I asked my students to write short stories about Ramadan. I also requested that they write poems about the Quran, Ramadan, Eid, the Prophet Muhammad (pbuh), and thankfulness.

I then worked on developing creative art projects to bring to life Islamic ideals and help us celebrate Islamic holidays.

Not only did we relate existing arts and crafts projects to Islam, but we also created new ideas and taught the students to relate everything we used to the One who created the materials: Allah. We taught them that all man-made items are ultimately natural creations by Allah's.

As an example, we asked the students what wax is made of and encouraged them to do their research and come back to class with an answer. "Wax is made from natural things like cattle fat, sugars, and honey," they wrote. Then we asked them what people use wax for. "People use wax for things like crayons, candles, and cosmetics," they'd answer. We wanted to clarify to the students that by using their creativity and Allah's creations, they could produce beautiful art!

Then, from 2011 to 2021, I worked to publish children's books. I developed these books for children: Ramadan Stories, Islamic Poems, Islamic Arts & Crafts Projects, All About Allah, All About Prophet Musa, and All About Prophet Muhammad. They are available at:

www.Islam4families.com

I hope my story will encourage other parents to work with their local communities to inspire their children to be proud of and to use their resources to develop their Muslim American identities.

~ *Sahar Abdel-Aziz*

INTRODUCTION

Prophet Muhammad (570-632) is the Prophet of Islam. He was an important religious, political, and military leader who helped to unite Arabia under Islam. Whilst in seclusion in a mountain cave, Muhammad received a series of revelations from God; these revelations form the verses of the Quran, which is the Word of God and around which the Islamic religion is based.

Prophet Muhammad was born in 570 CE in the Arabian city of Mecca. Orphaned from an early age, he was brought up first by his grandfather and then by his uncle Abu Talib. In his early life, he worked as a merchant and shepherd. Muhammad had spiritual inclinations and would spend time going to caves around Mount Hira to remain in silence, prayer and retreat.

It was during one of these retreats that he later revealed hearing the voice of Angel Jibreel (Gabriel). Muhammad shared these recitations with his wife and close companions who later served as scribes, writing down the revelations.

In the beginning, he attracted a relatively small number of followers, who were viewed with hostility by others in Mecca. In 622, as a result of the persecuation of the Muslims, Muhammad, with some of his followers, migrated to Medina. This migration is known as the Hijrah and marks the beginning of the Islamic calendar. In Medina, Muhammad united various tribes and with his growing political and religious strength was able to successfully fight the opposing tribes of Mecca. Eventually, Muhammad was able to lead 10,000 followers to the city of Mecca, where he was able to establish Islam within the city. During the remainder of his life, he was able to unite most of Arabia under the new religion of Islam, and also under a common political entity. Muhammad died in 632.

We are taught of the blessings that come with repeating the phrase, "May God's peace and blessings be upon him," upon mention of the Prophet Muhammad's name. We use "Muhammad" and "Prophet Muhammad" interchangeably throughout this book. As we do so, we send God's peace, blessings, and mercy upon the blessed Prophet and hope that you will do the same.

THE MAP OF ARABIA

CHAPTER 1: THE PROPHECY

Although poetry was an important part of Meccan culture, the majority of the people were illiterate. Most Meccans were traders that traveled from one place to another to sell their merchandise. One day, before the Prophet Muhammad was born, a few Arab men traveled to Syria as part of their usual trade route. On their way, they decided to stop by a group of monks who lived far away from Mecca in order to focus on worshipping God and reading scripture.

The Arabs often asked them questions and enjoyed hearing the enlightened responses from the monks who were known for their ability to read and their willingness to share stories from their books. When the monks learned that the Arab merchants were from Mecca, they said, "God will send you a Prophet from your people soon." The men were excited, as this would mean glory and greater power for their people, and each one wished that the forthcoming Prophet of God would be his son. The men asked the monks what the name of this Prophet would be and they responded, "His name will be Ahmed, and he will guide you to a new way of life."

QUESTIONS

1. What was the profession of the people of Mecca before Prophet Muhammad was born?
2. Why did the people of Mecca stop by the Monks on their way to Syria?
3. What did the Monks say to the Meccans when they found out they were from Mecca?
4. What did the Monks say the Prophet's name would be?
5. According to the monks, what would the new Prophet do?

The Quran Surah Al Fil (105:1-5):
1. Have you not considered how your Lord dealt with the People of the Elephant?
2. Did He not make their plan go wrong?
3. He sent against them swarms of birds.
4. Throwing at them rocks of baked clay.
5. Leaving them like chewed-up leaves.

أَلَمْ تَرَ كَيْفَ فَعَلَ رَبُّكَ بِأَصْحَابِ الْفِيلِ ۝

أَلَمْ يَجْعَلْ كَيْدَهُمْ فِي تَضْلِيلٍ ۝

وَأَرْسَلَ عَلَيْهِمْ طَيْرًا أَبَابِيلَ ۝

تَرْمِيهِم بِحِجَارَةٍ مِّن سِجِّيلٍ ۝

فَجَعَلَهُمْ كَعَصْفٍ مَّأْكُولٍ ۝

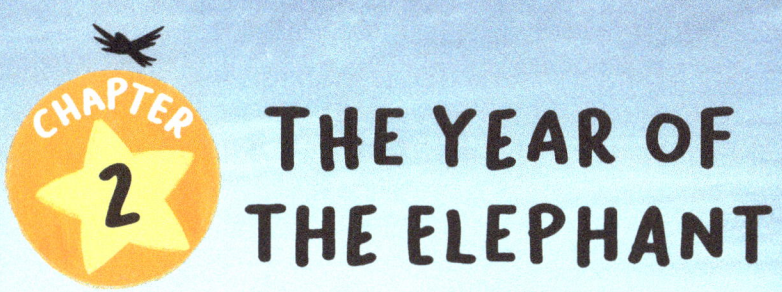

THE YEAR OF THE ELEPHANT

Before Prophet Muhammad was born, King Abraha ruled Abyssinia and conquered the country of Yemen in the Arabian Peninsula. He was a ruler who loved power and expected his people to obey and respect him. During his rule, the king learned that Mecca, which is close to his country of Yemen, had become an important and popular city because people traveled to visit a special building called the Kaaba to worship idols and gods. The Kaaba, rebuilt by Prophets Ibrahim and Ismail, is the first house of worship of God built on earth. The king decided to build a big beautiful decorative building in his country for people to worship instead of the Kaaba in Mecca. However, people continued to view the Kaaba as more sacred so they did not obey his orders to visit his new building. King Abraha grew angry and decided to take his large army, led by strong elephants, to Mecca to destroy the Kaaba so that people would be forced to go to his country to worship the building he built. When the people of Mecca heard about the strong army coming to attack their Kaaba, panic arose. They did not know how to protect the Kaaba and combat such a powerful army so they prayed to their gods for help and protection.

While the Meccans were trying their best to protect themselves, King Abraha's army of elephants continued heading towards Mecca. The king was confident that they had the strength and manpower to destroy the Kaaba, however once they were close to Mecca, the elephants miraculously refused to get closer or move from their spot. No matter how much they coaxed the elephants, they would not budge. The men discovered that when they guided the elephants in the opposite direction, they would walk, but when they urged them back to the direction of the Kaaba, they would stop in their spot. As the men continued to struggle with moving the elephants, a swarm of birds started to near. Soon thousands of birds carrying stones in their beaks flew on top of King Abraha's army and attacked the men, pelting them with the stones.

The army realized that the elephants' and the birds' reactions were no coincidence and that there was a greater power protecting the Kaaba. They redirected the elephants away from Mecca and fled back to their country, never to return. This event was very memorable to the Meccans because they knew that it was God who protected their place of worship. This year was referred to as "The Year of the Elephant," a year that is shaped not only by the miraculous actions of the animals, but also by the birth of a special baby boy named Muhammad who would grow up to be one of the most beloved Prophets of Islam.

ROUTE FROM ABYSSINIA TO KAABA

QUESTIONS

1. What is the name of Abraha's country?
2. What was the country close to Mecca which Abraha ruled?
3. What did Abraha build in his country and why?
4. Why did Abraha get angry and what did he do when he got angry?
5. What did the elephants do as they got closer to the Kaaba?
6. What did the thousands of birds do to Abraha's army?
7. Why did the people of Mecca thank God?
8. If the elephants could have talked, what do you think they would have said to Abraha?

CHAPTER 3: THE BIRTH OF THE PROPHET

Abdul Muttalib was an influential leader of the Arab tribe, "Quraysh," in Mecca. One day, he was asleep in the Kaaba and had a dream of a tree that was growing toward the sky with branches that spread East and West. In the dream, a bright light was shining on the tree and Arabs and people of other ethnic backgrounds were bowing to the tree or chopping off its branches and holding them. Abdul Muttalib woke up frightened from such an absurd dream. He decided to go to the priest, as was their custom at the time, to ask for advice and receive a spiritual interpretation. The priest reassured Abdul Muttalib that he should not be frightened. "If your dream comes true," the priest said, "then you will have a son who will control the East and the West, and people will follow him." The priest's words eased his mind and rather than worry, Abdul Muttalib felt a new peace.

Years passed and none of Abdul Muttalib's sons were leaders, however, he continued to wait for the son he was told would rule the East and the West. Meanwhile, Amina, the wife of his son, Abdullah, became pregnant. During this time, 570 CE, Abdullah, like many Meccans, was on a trading trip when he got sick and died. He was never able to meet his son. Amina was naturally saddened by the loss of her husband, yet she felt strong throughout her pregnancy. She had several dreams when she was pregnant that foreshadowed the blessed nature of the son she would bear. In one of her dreams, she saw a bright light. In another, Amina heard a voice that said to her, "Amina, you are carrying the greatest man in the world. Name him Muhammad, which means 'the praised one.'"

Amina gave birth to a baby boy. Remembering the blessed dream, she named the baby Muhammad, even though this name had never been used before. There were many signs that marked the day Prophet Muhammad was born. Some Jewish scholars were expecting another Prophet as mentioned in their scriptures. One of these men saw a brilliant new star that he had never seen before as he studied the heavens that night. He knew that the new star was a sign that a Prophet was born. The same night, another Jewish man passed by the meeting place of the leaders of Quraysh and asked them if a baby boy had just been born. When they replied with, "yes," the man explained that this boy will be the Prophet of the Arab nations. When Amina gave birth, she was in Mecca. Since her husband had died, Amina sent a message to her father-in-law, Abdul Muttalib, informing him about his new grandson Muhammad. He was elated to hear the news and loved the unique name; he prayed for his new grandson to grow up to be the greatest man on Earth.

Abdul Muttalib announced the birth of his grandson and presented him to the people of Mecca. He slaughtered sheep and had a feast for the community, the custom to show gratitude. Since the name Muhammad was never heard before, many people questioned why Abdul Muttalib's grandson had such a unique name. He answered the Meccans by saying that he wanted Muhammad to be praised in Heaven and on Earth. Prophet Muhammad, peace be upon him, was born an orphan but would become a messenger chosen by God to lead humanity on a brighter path. He is the manifestation of Prophet Ibrahim's prayer from many generations before.

The Quranic verse: "Our Lord, make a messenger of their own rise up from among them, to recite Your revelations to them, teach them the Scripture and wisdom, and purify them: You are the Mighty, the Wise." (2:129)

رَبَّنَا وَابْعَثْ فِيهِمْ رَسُولًا مِّنْهُمْ يَتْلُو عَلَيْهِمْ آيَاتِكَ وَيُعَلِّمُهُمُ الْكِتَابَ وَالْحِكْمَةَ وَيُزَكِّيهِمْ ۚ إِنَّكَ أَنتَ الْعَزِيزُ الْحَكِيمُ ﴿١٢٩﴾

QUESTIONS

1. What was the name of Prophet Muhammad's mother?
2. What was the name of Prophet Muhammad's grandfather?
3. What did Abdul Muttalib do when he was disturbed by his dream and how did he feel about it?
4. How did Amina feel when she was pregnant?
5. What did the voice in Amina's dream tell her?
6. What does Muhammad mean?

CHAPTER 4: HALIMA AND HER BLESSING

Halima, a bedouin woman from the Bani Sa'd tribe, was poor, and life was difficult for her and her family. One year in particular was a struggle because their donkey that she used for travel was too hungry and weak and their camel did not provide milk for them. Struggling with poverty, she did not eat well and could not even nurse her newborn baby. One day, Halima went to Mecca with her husband and newborn son to offer her services as a wet nurse and caretaker for a baby as a means of making a living. It was the custom in Mecca to send newborn children outside the city to the desert to spend their early days in cleaner air and a healthier environment. Halima thought this would be a way for her and her family to earn money for their survival. Since she was not able to nurse her own child, she was skeptical that she would be able to nurse another, but she decided to try because her family needed the money.

Halima was not the only woman from the desert to offer her services to families in Mecca. Most women found jobs among families that could guarantee generous payments. Many were unwilling to take Muhammad, because they assumed they wouldn't be paid well, since the child was an orphan.

However Halima, who was unable to find work anywhere else, agreed to nurse and raise Muhammad in her home in the desert, despite expecting a small payment. She knew she could not go back home empty handed so she prayed for blessings for her family because she was taking care of an orphan child.

After she assumed responsibility of the child, Halima experienced blessing after blessing. As soon as she started nursing him, her health became significantly better and she was able to nurse both Muhammad and her own son. When she and her husband arrived home, they noticed that their land was turning green and the date trees looked healthier. Their camel, which was severely malnourished when they left, began to produce milk again. The two sensed that all the positive changes in their life happened because of this blessed baby Muhammad. After the agreed upon years passed, it was difficult for Halima and her husband to part with Muhammad, whom they loved and cared for so much.

"Did We not relieve your heart for you, and remove the burden that weighed so heavily on your back, and raise your reputation high? So truly where there is hardship there is also ease; truly where there is hardship there is also ease. So when you are free, work on and direct your requests to your Lord." (94:1-8)

اَلَم نَشرَح لَكَ صَدرَكَ ۞
وَوَضَعنَا عَنكَ وِزرَكَ ۞
الَّذى اَنقَضَ ظَهرَكَ ۞
وَرَفَعنَا لَكَ ذِكرَكَ ۞
فَاِنَّ مَعَ العُسرِ يُسرًا ۞
اِنَّ مَعَ العُسرِ يُسرًا ۞
فَاِذَا فَرَغتَ فَانصَب ۞
وَاِلى رَبِّكَ فَارغَب ۞

QUESTIONS

1. Who is Halima?
2. Why did Halima go to Mecca?
3. What happened to Halima after she took baby Muhammad to the desert?
4. What did Halima not want to give back baby Muhammad to his mom?

CHAPTER 5: MUHAMMAD'S FIRST MERCHANT TRIP

As a child, Muhammad lived with his mother, Amina, in Mecca. One day, Amina decided to take her son to Yathrib, later known as Medina, to visit his uncle. There, he would have the chance to learn how to swim, fly kites, and play with his cousins in the cooler weather. It was the perfect place for Muhammad to spend part of his childhood and after such a long time in Yathrib, it was difficult for him to leave. Eventually, it was time for Muhammad to travel the long journey back to Mecca with his mother and their servant, Barakah. During the journey, Amina became ill and died. She was buried in a little town close to Yathrib called Al Abwa. Suddenly, Muhammad, at only age six, found himself returning home to Mecca without a mother or a father. However, his grandfather, Abdul Muttalib, took him in and loved him dearly. He saw his late son in Muhammad and knew that he would grow up to be the important person from his dream who would rule the East and the West.

As a member of the Quraysh tribe, Abdul Muttalib would always take Muhammad along to the Kaaba. There, many people would ask Abdul Muttalib questions and ask for his advice as an elder. Muhammad enjoyed joining his grandfather at the Kaaba and watching him share his wisdom with the people. However, when Muhammad was only eight years old, his grandfather, whom he loved very much, got sick.

Afraid that his grandson would be alone when he died, Abul Muttalib told his son, Abu Talib, to make sure to take care of his nephew Muhammad. Sadly, Abdul Muttalib's death came soon after, and Abu Talib stayed true to his word and adopted Muhamamd into his family, where he would grow up alongside his cousins.

Abu Talib was a merchant like many Meccans. When Muhammad was around 12 years old, Abu Talib decided to take him on his first merchant trip to Syria. During their journey, they made a customary stop to visit the monks that lived North of Mecca. The monks were wise people who read scriptures and knew that another Prophet would come after Jesus. Bahira, a Christian monk in that area, saw the caravan coming from far away and he sensed that there was something different and miraculous about the approaching caravan of merchants. He noticed a large cloud just above the caravan that followed and protected them from the harsh desert sun. When the merchants arrived, Bahira invited them all for a feast, where they talked and listened to the monk's stories. He was searching for signs of a prophet among the people he was welcoming, but did not find what he was looking for.

17

He asked the people, "Is your whole caravan here, or did you leave someone behind?" The Meccans replied, "There is a young boy watching our camels." Bahira then insisted that the boy come to the feast too. When Muhammad arrived, the monk watched his manners and his appearance and realized that they fit the description in the old manuscripts about the new prophet. He then took Muhammad aside and asked him some questions about the Kaaba and the idols and tested him by trying to have Muhammad swear by the idols as the Arabs usually did. However, Muhammad was honest and said what came naturally to him; he explained to the monk that there was nothing he hated more than the idols. At that point, it was clear to Bahira that Muhammad was the coming Prophet. When he discovered that he was the nephew of Abu Talib, Bahira took him aside and told him to care for the boy, for he is "the praised one,"

QUESTIONS

1. Where did Amina take her son on a trip?
2. What happened to Amina on her way back to Mecca?
3. When Muhammad became an orphan with no mother or father, who took care of him?
4. How did the monk know there was a prophet with the caravan?
5. What did the monk tell Abu Talib?

CHAPTER 6: MUHAMMAD AND KHADIJA

Before Prophet Muhammad became the prophet we love, he was an orphan, taken in by his grandfather and uncle and raised to be an honest and strong man. His integrity was well known and admired, which inspired Khadija, a successful business woman who inherited her fortune from her wealthy Quraysh family, to hire Muhammad. Khadija, also known as Tahira, "the pure one", was not only known for her wealth but for her beauty, piety, and virtue. She admired the prophet's honesty and trusted him to sell her merchandise in Syria; she even sent her servant, Maysarah, to accompany Muhammad as he joined a caravan of traders from Mecca.

In Syria, Muhammad did business differently than the other merchants by placing his merchandise without prices. Instead, he told the customer how much the merchandise was worth and left it up to the customer to decide what they thought they were able to pay. This creative and fair method of business astonished buyers because they were not accustomed to such an honest seller who would not cheat them. His items sold more quickly and with a substantial profit because people trusted Muhammad.

Maysarah was pleasantly surprised to see a new way of conducting business. On their way back from Syria, he suggested to Muhammad that he go straight to Khadija to break the news. Khadija was not only pleased to hear that her merchandise was all sold but that the sales were conducted with such honesty and fairness. She knew Muhammad was a noble man and his actions confirmed her belief. At this time, Khadija was a widow and a mother from two previous marriages. Since she was a rich woman, many men wanted to marry her, however she was waiting to choose a noble and honest man for her family. When she heard about Muhammad's character she believed he was the man for her even though he was younger and had never been married.

Days passed and Khadija decided she wanted to send her servant to both Muhammad and his uncle Abu Talib to ask Muhammad to marry her. He agreed and was happy to be married to such an honest woman. After their marriage, Muhammad continued to work for Khadija and maintained his humble lifestyle by caring for the poor, the weak, and the orphans. Khadija was very happy to be married to such an honest man whom she could trust to share her money with as well as to take care of their community. Together they offered Abu Talib, who was struggling to care and support his many children, a home for one of his sons, Ali. Abu Talib was very grateful and Ali soon became a part of Muhammad and Khadija's family. The couple had six other children together. They had four girls: Zaynab, Ruqayyah, Umm Kalthum, and Fatimah, as well as two boys: Qasim and Abdullah. Muhammad also adopted a boy named Zayd ibn al Harithah. His blessed family was known to love and serve their community and they continued to live a peaceful life. However, the couple did experience the loss of two of their children early on. Their two boys, Qasim and Abdullah, died young.

QUESTIONS

1. What quality was Muhammad known for?
2. True or False? The concept of integrity entails the value of truth, the truth in all things.
3. Who hired Muhammad and why?
4. How did Muhammad sell his merchandise?
5. Why was Khadija happy after the caravan came back ?
6. What qualities convinced Khadija to marry Muhammad?
7. What were the names of the 2 boys who lived with Khadija and Muhammad?
8. How many children did Khadija and Muhammad have together?

CHAPTER 7: THE BLACK STONE

Prophet Muhammad, Khadija, and their children lived a peaceful life in Mecca. When the Prophet was a boy, Bahira, a monk, told his uncle to take care of him because he would grow to be a special man that would change the history of the world. The Prophet was well known as Al Amin, the Truthful One, and a number of incidents happened to show that Bahira was right. Muhammad belonged to the Quraysh tribe in Mecca. Quraysh was in charge of the Kaaba, which was the first house of worship established on Earth. The Kaaba was rebuilt by Prophet Ibrahim and his son Prophet Ismail. By the time of Muhammad, the original message of Prophet Ibrahim was lost; the holy sanctuary of the Kaaba became filled with hundreds of idols and mixed with the traditions of pilgrims and travelers from distant places who were accustomed to idol worship and mythology.

The black stone, placed in one of the corners of The Kaaba, was considered holy to all the tribes of Mecca. Even though people were not worshiping the One God, the God of Ibrahim, the Kaaba was still very important to them and it was considered to be a holy place where people performed pilgrimage in their own way.

The tribal leaders argued over which leader should have the honor of placing the Black Stone in its place. A wise man suggested a solution to this dilemma: The next person to approach the area of the Kaaba would decide for them who should place the stone.

As they waited, they were happy to see a man approach the Kaaba and were even happier when they recognized this man as Muhammad, the well-known businessman from the Quraysh tribe. They knew he was a fair and honest man who would make a wise and reasonable decision. The old wise man explained to Muhammad the situation. Muhammad asked them to bring a cover, spread it out on the ground, put the black stone in the middle of the cover, and have a man from each group hold an edge and lift the cover together to put the black stone in its place. This way, they would each have participated in the placing of the stone. The men were satisfied with this decision and agreed to stop fighting and to take Muhammad's advice. Once the men reached the corner of The Kaaba with the cover, the Prophet placed the stone in its place with his hands. Although this decision seemed simple, they had not thought of this compromise before. Muhammad was able to mediate and allow them each to contribute.

QUESTIONS

1. What was in The Kaaba that is different from when Prophet Ibrahim built it?
2. What was the dilemma Quraysh was going through?
3. Why were the groups happy when they saw a man approaching The Kaaba?
4. Why were they happy to see Muhammad?
5. What was the solution to the fighting?

CHAPTER 8: CAVE HIRA

Throughout his life, the Prophet had been protected and prepared by God for prophethood. He was given a good character and a desire for understanding life's questions. The Prophet Muhammad not only valued his relationships with his wife, Khadija, and his children, but also with his companions from different tribes in Mecca. The Prophet was known as "the honest one;" he valued meditation and the message of peace within oneself and one's community. Meditation was a common practice among Prophet Ismail's descendants and Prophet Muhammad would regularly go on meditation trips to cave Hira outside of Mecca. He would leave his family for days and sometimes for weeks and only pack dates, water, and bread for survival. During his meditations, The Prophet would ponder the universe and life itself and would often return to his wife with stories of his experiences and dreams in the cave.

Although Khadija feared for her husband while he was alone in the cave, she supported his trips for fifteen years because she knew he valued the peace he gained away from the corrupted city. The Prophet's experiences in the cave would ultimately prepare him for prophethood and the role to come.

QUESTIONS

1. Why Did Khadija support his meditation?
2. Where did Muhammad go to think and meditate?
3. What did Muhammad think about while meditating?

CHAPTER 9: THE FIRST REVELATION

Prophet Muhammad was 40 years old when he received the revelation of the first verse, or Aya, from the Quran. One night during the month of Ramadan, Prophet Muhammad was meditating at Cave Hira when he heard a voice that said to him, "Read!" Not seeing anyone there, Muhammad was scared and said back to the voice, "I do not know how to read." The voice said again, "Read!" Muhammad said again, while in fear, "I cannot read." The powerful voice said, once again, "Read!" Muhammad asked, "What shall I read?" The beautiful voice revealed the next verses of the Quran:

"Read! In the name of your Lord who created: He created humans from a clinging form. Read! Your Lord is the Most Bountiful One who taught by the pen, who taught humankind which they did not know." (96:1-5).

اقْرَأْ بِاسْمِ رَبِّكَ الَّذِي خَلَقَ ۝
خَلَقَ الْإِنْسَانَ مِنْ عَلَقٍ ۝
اقْرَأْ وَرَبُّكَ الْأَكْرَمُ ۝
الَّذِي عَلَّمَ بِالْقَلَمِ ۝
عَلَّمَ الْإِنْسَانَ مَا لَمْ يَعْلَمْ ۝

Through these verses of the Quran, Prophet Muhammad was commanded by God to be a messenger and continued to receive revelation of verses over a period of twenty-three years until the religion was completed and the Prophet's life on earth ended. The Prophet sometimes received a few verses and other times, entire chapters. Some revelations came down in response to an inquiry, while some came for more knowledge about lessons from the past, and others included new teachings about God, the Hereafter, or dealings with other people.

After Prophet Muhammad received the first Ayas, his fear was apparent; his face was sweating and his heart was beating fast. He didn't know what this visit meant.

He ran down the mountain and heard the voice telling him, "Oh Muhammad, you are the messenger of God, and I am the Angel Gabriel." Everywhere he turned, Muhammad saw the angel. He continued to run to his beloved wife, Khadija, for security and comfort. Shivering, he asked her to cover him. Prophet Muhammad struggled to fully grasp the surreal experience. Was it an evil spirit, he wondered, or was he losing his mind? Khadija gently comforted him as he explained what had just happened. She calmly responded, "God will never disgrace you. You are a good man with God. You keep good relations with all your relatives, you help the poor and the needy, you serve your guests generously and assist the deserving unfortunate ones." She reminded him of his good character and realized that she knew someone who could help them make sense of this situation.

Khadija took Muhammad to her cousin, a learned scribe named Waraqah Bin Nawfal, who knew the Torah and the Gospel well. After they explained what took place at Hira, the old man, without hesitation, affirmed that this must have been a meeting with Angel Gabriel whom God had sent to Moses. He calmly told them that Muhammad was the chosen one they had all been waiting for. He also said, "I wish I were young and would live until the time when your people turn you away so that I could protect and follow you." He knew that the prophet foretold in the earlier scriptures had arrived, and that some would accept his message but others would reject it. Waraqah died before the Prophet Muhammad began to preach the message.

So began the call of the last Prophet, which was to influence the world forevermore and bring about a new age in the history of human consciousness with the birth of Islam. The first few people who followed the message were his wife Khadija, his daughters, his cousin Ali, his servant, his closest friend Abu Bakr, and later his adopted son Zayd Ibn Harithah. They all accepted Islam by acknowledging God as the only one worthy of worship and Prophet Muhammad as the last Prophet after Prophet Ibrahim and all the prophets of God. As soon as the revelation was received by Prophet Muhammad, he recited it to his close companions. Verses were written on different materials, including leather, palm leaves, and bark. It was written in Arabic, the language in which it was recited. Some companions also memorized the verses as soon as they heard them. The Quran was revealed over a period of twenty-three years from the year 609CE, when Prophet Muhammad was 40 years old, until the year 632CE, when Prophet Muhammad died at the age of 63.

Prophet Muhammad was a father, a husband, a friend, and a statesman. His impeccable character made him compassionate and merciful to all, even those who pledged to harm him. God taught him through the Quran how to deal with challenging circumstances. The mission of Prophet Muhammad was to restore the worship of the One God, as was taught by all the prophets before him. Islam means peace by submission and obedience to the will and commandments of God. Those who accept Islam are called Muslims.

QUESTIONS

1. How old was Prophet Muhammad when the Angel Gabriel visited him the first time?
2. The Quran was revealed over how many years?
3. Who was the first person who believed in Islam?
4. Who was the first youth who believed in Islam?
5. What does Islam mean?

CHAPTER 10: THE PERSECUTION OF MUSLIMS IN MEDINA

For 3 years after the revelations started, Prophet Muhammad preached God's words in secrecy. These words included reinforcements of the oneness of God, stories of the prophets before Muhammad, the rewards and punishments of the Hereafter, and the ways to achieve reward in this life and the next. Very few people accepted Islam during this time. However the ones who did varied in age and class for Islam is meant for everyone. After 3 years, the Prophet received revelation that he should go public and preach Islam to everyone. He then began to recite the revelations to people in public and invite them to a life of submission to the All-Powerful and Most Gracious God. He continued patiently to invite people to the basic pillar of Islam, which was to bear witness that there was no god but one God and that he, Muhammad, was the messenger of God.

> "Say, He is God the One, God the eternal. He begot no one nor was He begotten. No one is comparable to Him." (112:1-4).
>
> قُلْ هُوَ اللَّهُ أَحَدٌ ۝
> اللَّهُ الصَّمَدُ ۝
> لَمْ يَلِدْ وَلَمْ يُولَدْ ۝
> وَلَمْ يَكُن لَّهُ كُفُوًا أَحَدٌ ۝

The leaders of Quraysh did not like Muhammad's preaching of a belief in one God. This threatened their existing way of life and that of their forefathers. It was also a threat to the power structures and the status quo of their society. People who did not accept the message also questioned how Muhammad came up with these miraculous new words, so poetic in nature, while he himself had never learned to read or write, like many others in Mecca.

The Quraysh leaders became more and more enraged and asked him to stop preaching, but he did not. Leaders of Quraysh offered him money, position and power, but nothing would convince him to stop teaching others about the words of God. They wanted to get rid of him, but his uncle, Abu Talib, a powerful man in Quraysh, protected him. The Prophet said to Quraysh, "If they were to put the sun in my right hand and the moon in my left hand to stop me from spreading the message of Islam, I would never stop. I will keep preaching until God makes Islam prevail or I die."

Of course, the leaders of Quraysh were very upset to see their friends and family accepting the message. They thought the only way to stop the Muslims from following the new religion was to persecute them by beating and torturing them and boycotting their businesses. Many Muslims were publicly tortured. The first person who died as a result of this torture was a Muslim woman named Sumayya, also known as Umm Ammar. Bilal, an Abyssinian slave who became a Muslim, was also tortured by his master, who laid him in sand and placed a large, heavy rocks on his chest until he renounced Islam. He did not renounce his belief in the One God, and famously repeated the phrase "ahadun, ahad," or "One God, One God." People publicly humiliated the Prophet by throwing trash on him while walking in the street or while praying at the Kaaba. Despite the humiliation, persecution, and torture, Islam was growing and more people were becoming Muslims because of its message of the oneness of God, goodness to others, and the beautiful character of Prophet Muhammad.

In the fifth year of Islam, when the persecution was becoming unbearable for most Muslims, the Prophet advised people to emigrate to Abyssinia, a place known for being more tolerant due to its just leader. The Quraysh went after the Muslims who emigrated to bring them back to persecute them. However, after Negus, the Christian leader of Abyssinia, investigated the Muslims' belief and heard the Quranic revelation about Jesus and Mary, peace be upon them both, he granted the Muslims protection. Since the Quraysh were no longer able to bring back the Muslims who emigrated, they continued and worsened the humiliation of Muslims in Mecca.

The Prophet insisted that if the people of Quraysh had the freedom to practice their religion, then the Muslims should have the freedom to practice Islam. The Prophet recited the chapter that ends with the words:

> You have your religion and I have mine" (109:6).
>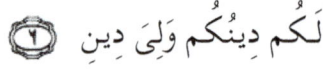

Quraysh implemented a total ban on contact with the Prophet's family which lasted for three years.

During the persecution, the Prophet was sad because of the passing of his first supporter and first believer in Islam, his beloved wife Khadija. Soon after the ban was lifted, he also lost his uncle, Abu Talib, who was his great supporter and protector. This was a very sad year of his life and it would go on to be known as The Year of Sadness.

After the death of Prophet Muhammad's wife and uncle, he went to Taif to seek protection. There, he was chased out of the city by children who threw garbage and stones at him. As the Prophet left the city upset, Angel Gabriel came down to visit him and send a message. The angel told the Prophet that he had the choice to make a prayer that would destroy the town as punishment for what they did to him. Prophet Muhammad declined and instead prayed for future generations of Taif to accept Islam. He took his sadness and humiliation to God and asserted that if God was pleased with him, then nothing else mattered.

It was a challenging time in the Prophet's life due to the persecution of the Muslims in Mecca, not being accepted at Taif, and the sadness over the loss of both his beloved wife and his uncle who protected him since the start of the revelation.

Soon after these incidents, God took Prophet Muhammad on a unique journey called the Israa and the Miraaj. This is where Angel Gabriel took Prophet Muhammad miraculously from the sacred house of worship near the Kaaba to the furthest Masjid in Jerusalem, Al Aqsa, in a very short time in the middle of the night. On this journey the Prophet met with previous prophets, Abraham, Moses, Jesus and many more, whom he had the chance to lead in prayer. He was reminded of the great legacy of messengers and prophets of which he was a part. Angel Gabriel then took the Prophet to Heaven with God's permission. This is where the Prophet met with the previous prophets and the five daily prayers were prescribed. He was then taken back to the Kaaba. The entire experience lasted one night.

When he told people what happened, many of them scoffed at and made fun of him. When he described the things he saw and people he met, some people recognized that although the story seemed physically impossible, the Prophet Muhammad was known to be a person who never lied, and they believed the story as a miracle and gift from God. His companion Abu Bakr was one of the people who believed him immediately, and it was then that he earned the title, Al-Siddiq, or "the truthful."

This is when Quraysh decided that they had had enough of Prophet Muhammad and that they wanted him killed. They planned to pick men from Quraysh to attack the Prophet. However God revealed this information to the Prophet, and he waited for a revelation on what to do next. The Angel Gabriel instructed the Prophet to leave Mecca.

However, Prophet Muhammad, who was trustworthy, planned to leave as soon as he returned all the items that other people had entrusted him with. Meanwhile, he instructed some Muslims to leave and migrate to Medina first.

Prophet Muhammad planned with a guide the best way to leave Mecca. The guide suggested that they travel South of Mecca even though Medina is toward the North in order to trick the Quraysh, who would certainly follow him when they found out that he had left. Prophet Muhammad asked Ali, his cousin, to sleep in his bed so no one would notice that he left his bed during the night, which would give him more time to start his journey away from Mecca. He also picked Abu Bakr, his close friend, to travel with him. The Prophet's migration strategy included choosing a person who would update them on the Quraysh's whereabouts as well as choosing Abu Bakr's daughter, Asma, to bring them food while he and her father hid in Cave Thawr. The Prophet and Abu Bakr hid for three nights until they heard that the coast was clear for them to travel North to Medina.

QUESTIONS

1. How many years did Prophet Muhammad preach Islam in secrecy?
2. What did Prophet Muhammad say to the Quraysh when they told him to stop preaching?
3. Who was the first Muslim woman who died in persecution?
4. Why did Quraysh want to kill Prophet Muhammad?
5. What was the name of the cave where Prophet Muhammad was hiding?

The long journey from Mecca to Medina became known as the Hijra, or "migration," which marks the first year of the Muslim calendar. Finally, Prophet Muhammad and Abu Bakr were approaching Medina, which was known as Yathrib at the time. Islam had already spread to Medina by the Jewish community and adopted by some in the Aws and Khazraj tribes before the Prophet's arrival. However, many people were still excited to meet the well-known Prophet in person and hear more of the new religion which was a continuation of the traditions of the prophets before him.

As Prophet Muhammad was getting close to Medina, he stopped in the town of Quba and began building the foundation of the first Masjid with the believers. Today, praying at the Masjid in Quba is said to carry the same reward as performing Umrah.

In Medina, Muslims were finally free to worship and practice their religion. Upon arrival to the city, many offered the beloved Prophet their homes for him to stay in because they wanted the chance to host the Prophet and learn from him. The Ansar, the supporters in Medina, kept their promise to protect the Prophet when he arrived and treat the Muhajarin, the migrants from Mecca, like their family. Because of their persecution in Mecca, many Muhajirin arrived in Medina without money and property but the Ansar supported them as brothers and sisters in faith.

To ensure peace and tranquility, the Prophet proposed a treaty defining terms of conduct for all inhabitants of Medina, which included Muslims and those of other faiths. This document insured mutual respect and protection for one another. As time passed, more Muslims fled the persecution of Mecca in secrecy and migrated to Medina without their properties to create a peaceful life for themselves and their families.

QUESTIONS

1. What was the journey from Mecca to Medina called?
2. When did the first year of the Muslim calendar start?
3. Who traveled with Prophet Muhammad from Mecca to Medina?
4. What was Medina called in the old days?
5. What was the name of the original residents of Medina?
6. What was the name of the people who moved to Medina?

Pillars of Islam and Call to Prayer

While building the Masjid in Medina, the Prophet Muhammad wondered how to call believers to prayer. Christians called each other to pray by striking wooden clappers together. Jewish people called their believers for prayer by blowing a ram's horn. The Prophet wanted a unique and memorable way to call Muslims to prayer so he consulted with his companions and they all agreed that the beautiful, God-given human voice was the best way to call one another for prayer. The call for prayer is translated into:

"God is most great, God is most great. I bear witness that there is no god but God. I bear witness that Muhammad is the Messenger of God. Come to prayer. Come to success. God is most great, God is most great. There is no God but God."

☆ اَللّٰهُ اَكْبَرْ ☆ اَللّٰهُ اَكْبَرْ ☆	☆ اَللّٰهُ اَكْبَرْ ☆ اَللّٰهُ اَكْبَرْ ☆
☆ اَشْهَدُاَنْ لَا اِلٰهَ اِلَّا اللّٰهُ ☆	☆ اَشْهَدُاَنْ لَا اِلٰهَ اِلَّا اللّٰهُ ☆
☆ اَشْهَدُاَنَّ مُحَمَّدًا رَسُوْلُ اللّٰهِ ☆	☆ اَشْهَدُاَنَّ مُحَمَّدًا رَسُوْلُ اللّٰهِ ☆
☆ حَيَّ عَلَى الصَّلٰوةِ ☆	☆ حَيَّ عَلَى الصَّلٰوةِ ☆
☆ حَيَّ عَلَى الْفَلَاحْ ☆	☆ حَيَّ عَلَى الْفَلَاحْ ☆
☆ لَا اِلٰهَ اِلَّا اللّٰهُ ☆	☆ اَللّٰهُ اَكْبَرْ اَللّٰهُ اَكْبَرْ ☆

Muslims wanted the call to prayer to sound beautiful, so the Prophet asked his companion, Bilal, who had a great voice, to say the first-ever prayer call. Bilal, a Black man, was once enslaved but freed during the early days of Islam by Abu Bakr. He agreed to learn the call and he became the first-ever Mu'ezzin, one who calls Muslims to prayer. It gave Bilal great honor to be personally chosen by the Prophet Muhammad to be the first Mu'ezzin of Islam.

As the pillars of the Masjid were built, so were the five foundational pillars of Islam:
1. Shahada: The belief in the following fundamental statement: I bear witness that there is no god but God and I bear witness that Muhammad is the messenger of God.
2. Salat: Five prayers per day as a means to connect with God throughout the day: Early morning prayer, noon prayer, afternoon prayer, sunset prayer and evening prayer.
3. Zakat: Contribution to be distributed to the poor from a person's wealth.
4. Fasting: Fasting from dawn to sunset during the month of Ramadan.
5. Hajj: The pilgrimage to the holy Masjid in Mecca, the Kaaba, following the footsteps of Prophet Ibrahim, as Prophet Muhammad taught us. This is done one time in a person's life only if s/he has the means to do so.

1. What is the name of the person who calls people for prayer?
2. Who was the first person who called people for prayer?
3. Why was the first person who called people for prayer picked?
4. How is building a Masjid similar to the pillars of Islam?

CHAPTER 13: LOVE AND LOSS

The Prophet was 60 years old and married to Mariyah, an Egyptian Christian, when their son, Ibrahim, died. No matter how busy the Prophet was as a leader, he always put time aside for his son, whom he loved dearly. One day, the Prophet came home to find his wife cradling their son as he laid still in her arms. With tears in his eyes, he immediately reached out for his son, and together Mariyah and the Prophet Muhammad held Ibrahim close as he died in their arms.

The Prophet remained with his wife to comfort and remind her that Ibrahim was in a much better place. He told her how he was now in heaven with God where he was safe and at peace. That day, an eclipse formed in the sky. The world grew dark for a moment, and many thought it was a bad omen from God, but the Prophet reassured them that the sun and the moon were too from God and will bring forth light soon. Much like coping with death, the world seems so dark in the moment, but one must remember that light will always follow.

His son's death caused much hurt and sadness for the Prophet. The pain of his loss was clear in his eyes and noted by anyone who passed him. Many surrounding Muslims became confused and wondered why the Prophet would openly display his emotions when he had earlier forbid excessive expressions of grief. The Muslims addressed their Prophet with their concerns and Prophet Muhammad clarified his message by explaining that feeling sadness is never forbidden. Although he advised against the unnecessary and hysterical wailing that was paired with loss, the Prophet encouraged embracing one's emotions because it is a natural and humbling act that shows the amount of love and empathy that is in the heart.

1. What lesson can be learned from the Eclipse that happened the day of Ibrahim's death?
2. What does the Prophet advise against when coping with loss?
3. How did the Prophet act when his son had died?

CHAPTER 14: THE PROPHET'S AIM FOR PEACE

As soon as Prophet Muhammad moved to Medina, he proposed a treaty to define the terms of conduct for all those who lived in the city, including the Muslims, the Jewish community, and people of other faiths. As time passed, people against Islam increased in the surrounding regions. After realizing that many Muslims had left Mecca, the people of Quraysh decided to act. They waged war against the Muslims in the battle of Badr. The Muslims were severely out numbered, however the Quran recounts that God sent angels to strengthen their army. This support allowed the Muslims to win the battle despite their small numbers.

The new battle, The Battle of Uhud, caused great loss for the Muslims. Not only did they Muslims lose the battle, but some of them disobeyed orders from the Prophet when they left their posts because it seemed that the Muslims were winning. However, it taught them an important lesson on unity and the danger of short sightedness. After the battle, the Prophet and a few Muslims wanted to perform Hajj, however, the Meccans took advantage of the Muslims' weakened state and prohibited them from entering Mecca. A few people from Quraysh approached them in Hudaybiyah, where they negotiated and signed a treaty that disallowed Hajj that year and prohibited Muslims in Mecca from going to Medina. However, the treaty promised peace and allowed Muslims from Medina to perform Hajj the following year. Many of the Prophet's companions did not understand why such a treaty was accepted and were angry for relenting and showing weakness. But the Prophet was wise and had a plan. The Prophet knew that a year of peace was important to allow the weakened Muslim community to develop and expand.

Meanwhile, as the community continued to grow, the Prophet sent letters to surrounding rulers to teach them about Islam. Many accepted his message, including the kings of Abyssinia and Bahrain, as well as the emperor Heraclius and Chakrawati Farmas, the Hindu king of Malabar.

Two years after the signing of the Treaty of Hudaybiyah, in 629CE, Quraysh violated the terms of the treaty by attacking Bani Khuzah, an ally of the Prophet. In response, the Prophet gathered the Muslims of Medina and surrounding regions and marched to Mecca. Before he entered Mecca, he announced that, "everyone remaining in their home, Abu Sufyan's home, or in the Kaaba will be safe." He and the Muslims then entered Mecca peacefully. The Prophet pointed at each of the idols at the Kaaba with his stick and said 'Truth has come and falsehood will fade away' and one by one, the idols fell down. All 360 idols were removed and the Kaaba was finally cleansed and restored to its pristine status as the House of Allah, just as it was when built by Prophets Ibrahim and Ismail.

Due to the Meccan's twenty years of persecution, torture, and war against the Muslims, they expected the Prophet, who now showed strength, to retaliate. They were surprised to be treated with compassion when the Prophet, standing by the Kaaba, promised them peace and said, "Oh Quraysh, what do you think I am about to do with you?" They replied, "Good. You are a noble brother, son of a noble brother."

The Prophet forgave them all and said, "I will treat you as Prophet Yousuf treated his brothers. There is no reproach against you. Go to your homes, and you are all free... Allah made Mecca holy today." He continued,

"He created the heavens and earth and it is the holiest of holy places until Resurrection Day. It is not lawful for anyone who believes in Allah and the last day to shed blood therein, nor to cut down trees therein. It was not lawful to anyone before me and it will not be lawful to anyone after me." Eventually, the people of Mecca and even the enemies of the Prophet accepted Islam.

1. Name two battles which took place around Medina.
2. What happened at Hudaybiyah?
3. What did Prophet Muhammad do when he entered Mecca?

Despite being the year that Prophet Muhamamd's son Ibrahim died, The Year of Delegations is a celebrated time because it is known for the great number of people converting to Islam. The religion became the stronghold for unifying Arabia and creating a powerful civilization.

By the following year, 630CE, almost all of Arabia had accepted Islam. The Prophet performed his first and final pilgrimage in 632 CE, alongside 120,000 men and women. It was during this time that he received his last revelation. The Prophet died two months later, on a Monday, 12 Rabi al Awwal, the eleventh year after Hijra to Medina. Some of his last words were, "We, the community of prophets, are not inherited. Whatever we leave is for charity." The Prophet was buried in his house where he died.

To this day, people visit the Prophet in Medina to pay their respects and send peace and blessings to him.

After returning from the Pilgrimage, the Prophet addressed his people, "Oh people, hear what I have to say to you, for I do not know whether I will meet you ever again after this year in this place."

He reminded his people to remain humble and compassionate for one another because all Muslims are brothers and sisters, regardless of race or ethnicity. He hoped that his message of equality would pass on to future followers and introduced the Quran to protect and help people remain on the right path. The Quran is God's words, guiding people to live a spiritual life that recognizes one God and benefits others.

The Prophet ended his speech with the final verses of the Quran:

> "...This day I have made perfect your religion for you and have completed my favor to you, and it has pleased me to give you Islam as your religion..." (5:3).
>
> ... اَلْيَوْمَ اَكْمَلْتُ لَكُمْ دِينَكُمْ وَاَ تَمَمْتُ عَلَيْكُمْ نِعْمَتِى وَرَضِيتُ لَكُمُ الْاِسْلَامَ دِينًا ... (٣)

Upon hearing these words, Abu Bakr, Prophet Muhammad's companion, started to cry. He knew that the Prophet's mission on Earth had come to an end and that Muslims would soon be on their own. They would have to learn how to live without their Prophet, a man who was a father, a brother, a friend, a leader, and the greatest man on Earth to all.

While on his deathbed, his daughter, Fatima, cried for her dying father until one night when he whispered in her ear and reassured her that she would be the next person to die after him and they will be reunited soon.

When the Prophet died at age 63, Fatima was his only living child left. She was married to Ali, a blessed companion to the Prophet, and together they had two boys, Husain and Hasan. The narrations are endless of the kindness and good character that the family possessed.

There is so much more to say about our Blessed and Beloved Prophet. He was merciful, loving, wise, and discerning. Everyone loved him. The Prophet always said that he was merely a man and, like every other man, he would one day die. However, when he did die, the Muslim community was hit hard with the realization that their lives must go on without him. When Abu Bakr heard the terrible news, he hurried to the Prophet's house to see for the last time the friend that he loved almost all his life.

He knew it was going to be hard for people to accept his death so he went out to comfort and talk to the people who were gathered to hear the news. He reassured everyone by saying, "O people, for those who worshipped Muhammad, Muhammad has died. But for those who worship God, God is living and does not die." Although the Messenger of God was dead, the message he brought to the world lives on.

May the blessing and peace of God be upon him.

QUESTIONS

1. What age was the Prophet when he died?
2. What did Prophet Muhammad whisper in Fatima's ears which made her smile?
3. What were two of Fatima's children's names?
4. List some lessons from the final sermon.

CHAPTER 16: THE MOST IMPORTANT MAN

Prophet Muhammad embodied the values of Islam and the characteristics taught in the Quran. He was also chosen by God to be one of the most important men in history. He was the messenger, a great husband, a compassionate friend, and a wise statesman. People who met Prophet Muhammad described him as handsome and intelligent. He was known to smile and greet people with a cheerful and welcoming face. The Prophet was rational and level headed; he did not let his emotions, like sadness and anger, get the best of him. He was a man who practiced what he preached and didn't like hypocrisy.

Prophet Muhammad was well-known to be the truthful and honest. He was just and merciful in dealing with others. He was a perfect role model. It is known for people to not only follow the teachings of the Quran and the Hadiths, but the Sunnah as well, which are the sayings, actions, and approvals of the Prophet.

He dressed like a simple man. He was very humble and accepted presents when offered but always gave them away to someone in need. The Prophet was very generous and encouraged generosity among his community. If he was given food, he would always share it with others. He taught that all people have the capacity to be generous, whether with their wealth, their time, or their kindness. Prophet Muhammad valued kindness and encouraged people to not only be kind to one another but to animals as well. He gave all of his animals names, including his camel, Qaswa, his horse, Sakb, and his mule, Duldul.

One of Prophet Muhammad's greatest teachings was for people to treat each other as brothers and sisters. He was always the first to start with greeting others. The Prophet always paid special and equal attention to people, whether they were rich, poor, young, old, strong or weak. In fact, many of his companions were convinced that they were the Prophet's favorite because of the full attention and care he paid to each of them.

1. Name 2 characteristics Prophet Muhammad was known for.
2. What did Prophet Muhammad do when he was given a gift?
3. What did Prophet Muhammad do when someone gave him food?
4. What was Prophet Muhammad's mule called?

APPENDIX
FACTS ABOUT THE MOTHERS OF THE BELIEVERS:

The women who were married to the Prophet Muhammad are known as Mothers of the Believers, a term derived from the Quran. In their lives are timeless lessons for all of humanity.

KHADIJA

Khadija was the daughter of Khuwaylid, a member of the Qurayshi and Asad tribes. She was a wealthy merchant in town and married the Prophet when she was forty years old and he was twenty-five. She was the Prophet's first wife and his only wife until she died. Together they had six children, four girls and two boys, however the boys both died in infancy. Khadija comforted the Prophet when he received his first revelation from God. She reminded him that God would protect him and reassured the Prophet that people will support him because of his great role in society. He protected his family, held great responsibility in the community, gave charity, honored guests, and was respected by everyone. She knew that people would trust him and supported her husband throughout his difficult early years of Prophethood where he was persecuted in Mecca and abused by the Qurayshi tribe. Khadija and Prophet Muhammad were married for twenty-five years. The Prophet always loved and respected Khadija. He deeply missed her when she died and left him with their four daughters. Khadija will always be remembered for her loving and supporting nature. God sent Khadija His greetings to her by name through the Angel Gabriel and promised her a special place in Paradise. In a hadith narrated by Al Bukhari we learn that Khadija was the best of women during her time.

SAWDA

Sawda was the daughter of Zam'a and one of the first converts to Islam who immigrated to both Abyssinia and Medina. When her first husband passed away in exile, Sawda became a poor widow raising her children alone. When she married the Prophet, they joined their families. Sawda was the first of a number of widows the Prophet married. She was married to Prophet Muhammad for three years until he asked for her approval to have another wife. Sawda was known for being a kind, charitable, and jovial woman.

AISHA

Aisha was the daughter of Abu Bakr, one of the Prophet's closest friends and later caliph of the Muslims after the Prophet's death. Aisha was raised as a Muslim and married the Prophet when she was very young. Aisha is mentioned in a verse of the Quran and was the only wife who was with the Prophet when he received a revelation. The Prophet died in Aisha's arms and after his death, she taught and played an important role in Islam for more than 40 years. Aisha was well known for her sharp intelligence and love of learning. She was among the most knowledgeable scholars and collected more than 2000 Hadiths. The Prophet's companions requested her opinion in religious matters and traveled far distances to learn from her.

HAFSA

Hafsa was the daughter of Umar ibn Al- Khattab, who was another one of the Prophet's closest friends and caliph of the Muslims after the Prophet's death. She immigrated with her first husband to both Abyssinia and Medina but became a widow at the age of 18. Her marriage to the Prophet was a political alliance and linked the Khattab family with the Prophet's family. Hafsa got along with Aisha well; they were both the youngest of the Prophet's wives. Hafsa was intelligent, strong, and a good writer. Like Aisha, she also memorized the entire Quran. After the death of her father, Hafsa had the great honor of being the custodian of the first Mushaf (Quran) when all the pages were compiled into a single book for the first time. Hafsa was married to the Prophet for eighteen years and lived for another thirty-four years after his death.

ZAINAB

Zainab was the daughter of Khuzayma ibn al Harith. Zainab had been widowed several times prior to her marriage to the Prophet. Her last husband, before her marriage to the Prophet, had died in a battle. Her marriage to the Prophet set a new precedent that removed the stigma against marrying widowed women during that time. Muslim men no longer feared that their deaths in battle would mean starvation and neglect for their families back home. It became honorable to marry the widows of the deceased, since the Prophet did so. She was also married to the Prophet's freed slave Zayd Ibn Haritha, who the Prophet treated like a biological son. Zainab and Zayd's marriage was short and ended in a divorce when they realized that this was best for both of them to be happy. Since divorce was not liked and it put the woman in a very difficult situation, God instructed the Prophet to marry Zainab instead. Zainab was always proud that God mentioned her in Surah Al Ahzab.

Additionally, the Prophet's marriage to Zainab demonstrated that the legal rulings of an adopted son are not the same as a biological son. Zainab is well known as the "Mother of the Poor" due to her exceeding generosity . Zainab died about two months after her marriage to Prophet Muhammad, which is why little else is known about her. She died when she was fifty years old.

UM SALAMAH

Um Salamah's real name was Hind bint Abi Umaya. She immigrated to Abyssinia with her first husband and they were also the first to immigrate to Medina. When her husband died, she made the following dua to Allah:

"O Lord, reward me for my affliction and give me something better than it in return, which only You, the Exalted and Mighty, can give."

Um Salamah was known for her great patience. She accompanied the Prophet in many expeditions and narrated 300 Hadith concerning women. She was married to the Prophet for seven years until his death and outlived all the other "Mothers of the Believers" and died at the age of eighty-four.

JUWAYRIYA

Juwayriya is the daughter of Al Haarith, the chief of the tribe Banu Mustaliq. She was captured in a battle against the tribe and her marriage to the Prophet brought alignment between her tribe and the Muslims. It allowed the tribe to enter Islam with honor by removing the humiliation of their defeat. As soon as the marriage was announced, all the war booties were returned to Banu Mustaliq and all the captives were set free. Juwayriya was married to the Prophet for 6 years and lived for 39 years after his death. She died at age 65.

UM HABIBA
(ALSO KNOWN AS RAMLA)

Um Habiba was the daughter of Abu Sufian Sakhr Ibn Harb from the Qurayshi tribes. She converted to Islam and suffered persistent oppression. She and her first husband joined the immigration to Abyssinia, however, she was later living in a foreign land with her young daughter when her husband died in Abyssinia. She accepted to marry the Prophet who offered to take care of her and her children. The king of Abyssinia provided her mahr and witnessed the marriage contract. She was married to the Prophet for 4 years before he passed away.

SAFIYA

Safiya was the daughter of Hyay Ibn Akhtab, the leader of Bany Nudair (a Jewish tribe) and a descendant of Aaron, brother of Musa. She was born in Medinah and settled at Khaybar where she was taken captive when the Muslims won the battle of Khaybar. She converted to Islam when she learned about the religion through the Prophet Muhammad. As a minority, she was often teased by other women about her Jewish background. In response, the Prophet Muhammad told her "Your husband is Muhammad, your father was Prophet Aaron, and your uncle was Prophet Musa. So what is there in that to be scornful about?" She was 21 years old when the Prophet died. She lived for another 39 years after the Prophet's death and died in Medina at 60 years old.

MARIA (BARRA)

Maria was the Daughter of Al Harith. She was a Christian slave from Egypt. She wanted to marry the Prophet so she offered herself to him in marriage and he accepted. She had one son, Ibrahim, who died in infancy. The Prophet was deeply saddened by Ibrahim's death. She lived with the Prophet for 3 years until he died.

PROPHET MUHAMMAD

A	O	A	i	B	A	R	A	L	U	E	A	A	G
H	Y	U	i	A	i	A	i	S	H	A	K	N	C
F	Y	T	i	R	A	H	C	K	Y	U	K	i	U
K	E	G	A	M	i	R	G	L	i	P	A	D	L
M	R	A	F	A	S	T	i	N	G	R	M	A	A
H	D	T	D	E	V	i	G	R	O	F	A	M	M
B	A	E	L	P	E	M	E	R	O	O	A	i	A
A	B	J	A	A	C	A	B	A	T	T	L	E	R
T	R	D	J	B	N	A	P	R	A	Y	E	R	R
i	E	U	S	A	E	A	i	A	N	A	O	i	i
H	N	H	C	A	L	H	i	R	A	A	H	C	A
C	i	U	R	K	i	C	O	M	M	A	N	D	G
i	R	J	E	R	S	H	A	L	L	A	i	i	E
H	Y	i	A	T	B	i	L	A	T	U	B	A	A

SILENCE · FASTING · BATTLE · COMMAND · AISHA
MARRIAGE · MAKKA · CHARITY · PILGRIMAGE · HIRA
FORGIVE · HAJJ · KAABA · ARABIA · MADINA
BADR · PRAYER · ABUTALIB · ALLAH · UHUD

ANSWERS:

Chapter 1:
1. Merchants   2. They were wise and well-read, and they enlightened people with their knowledge.
3. "God will send you a Prophet from your people soon."   4. Ahmed   5. Muhammad will guide you to a new way of life.

Chapter 2:
1. Abyssinia   2. Yemen   3. A big beautiful building for people to come to his country to worship
4. Because people were not coming to his country to worship the building he built, he decided to attack Mecca with the intent of destroying the Kaaba.   5. Refused to move toward the Kaaba   6. Threw stones at them   7. Because God protected the Kaaba   8. Free Response: The elephants did not obey orders to destroy The Kaaba.

Chapter 3:
1. Amina   2. Abdul Muttalib   3. Abdul Muttalib went to the priest to interpret the dream. The priest said to him, "Have no fear. If your dream comes true then you will have a son who will control the east and the west, and people will follow him."   4. Strong   5. You are carrying the greatest man in the world. Name your baby Muhammad.   6. The praised one

Chapter 4:
1. A poor woman from the desert from the Bani Sa'd tribe.   2. To get a baby to nurse so that she could earn some money for her family.   3. They were able to get milk from the camel, Halima was able to nurse her baby and baby Muhammad, the palm tree was full of dates, and the grass was green.   4. Halima and her family were blessed when baby Muhammad was with them and they loved him very much, it was very hard to give him back to his mom.

Chapter 5:
1. Yathrib (present day Madina)   2. She became ill and died.   3. His grandfather Abdul Muttalib
4. There was a cloud on top of the caravan protecting the caravan from the sun.   5. "Take care of Muhammad, for he is the praised one."

Chapter 6:
1. Muhammad was well known to be an honest young man who had integrity.   2. True   3. Khadija, because he was honest and had integrity   4. He placed merchandise out and informed the buyers of the value of the merchandise and then offered for them to pay what they could.   5. All the merchandise was sold with a profit.   6. Because he was honest and had integrity.   7. Ali and Zayd   8. 6 (2 boys who died very young and 4 girls).

Chapter 7:
1. There were a lot of idols that people were worshiping.   2. They all wanted to carry the black stone.
3. They were waiting for the first man who would solve their dilemma.   4. It was Muhammad who was known to be the honest, trustworthy and reasonable   5. Muhammad recommended spreading a cover out on the ground, putting the black stone in the middle of the cover, and having a man from each group hold the edge of the cover and lift the cover together at the same time and put it in its place.

Chapter 8:
1. She knew that he valued the peace he received from meditating.   2. Cave Hira   3. Life and the universe

Chapter 9:
1. 40 years old 2. 23 years   3. Prophet Muhammad's first wife Khadija   4. Prophet Muhammad's cousin Ali
5. Islam means submission and obedience to the will and commandments of God.

Chapter 10:
1. 3 years   2. If they were to put the sun in my right hand and the moon in my left hand to stop me from preaching Islam, I would never stop. I will keep preaching till Allah makes Islam prevail or I die.   3. The first Muslim who died was a Muslim woman called Umm Ammar or Summaya.   4. Quraysh wanted to kill Prophet Muhammad because he was preaching Islam.   5. The cave where Prophet Muhammad was hiding was called Hira.

Chapter 11:
1. Hijra   2. Hijra.   3. Abu Bakr   4. Yathrib   5. Ansar   6. Muhajirin

Chapter 12:
1. Mu'ezzin   2. Bilal   3. He had a strong, beautiful and powerful voice   4. Just like the pillars of the Masjid were built, the pillars of Islam was founded. A pillar is a support, and just like a pillar is a support for a building, the pillar of Islam is the support for Islam.

Chapter 13:
1. Much like coping with death, the world seems so dark in the moment, but one must remember that light will always follow.   2. He advised against the unnecessary and hysterical wailing that was paired with grief.
3. The Prophet remained with his wife to comfort and remind her that Ibrahim was in a much better place.

Chapter 14:
1. Battle of Badr and the battle of Uhud.   2. They negotiated a treaty allowing the Muslims to come back the following year for Hajj.   3. The Prophet pointed at each idol with his stick and said: 'Truth has come and falsehood will fade away' and one by one the idols fell down.' He also showed mercy to the people of Mecca.

Chapter 15:
1. 63   2. The Prophet told Fatima she would be the next person who would die after the Prophet's death and they would reunite.   3. Hasan and Husain   4. The religion is complete, Muslims are brothers and sisters regardless of race, the Quran is a guide for one's life

Chapter 16:
1. Truthful and Honest   2. He was humble and accepted the gift and he gave it away to someone in need
3. He shared it with others   4. His mule was called Duldul

www.ingramcontent.com/pod-product-compliance
Lightning Source LLC
Chambersburg PA
CBHW060857090426
42736CB00026B/3498